AKHENATEN
Son of the Sun

D.M. Alon

COPYRIGHT INFORMATION

Copyright © 11/01/2013 - Numinosity Press Incorporated

Published and distributed by: **Numinosity Press Inc**

Alon, Doron.

Akhenaten: Son of the Sun –1st ed

Printed in **Numinosity Press Inc**

ISBN: 0-9824722-8-5

Images used for Cover and content:
Cover Created by Shahnaz Mohammed
mailto:NAZNYC@GMAIL.COM
Alexander the Great © v0v - Fotolia.com
Joan Of Arc © Tupungato - Fotolia.com
Ghnegis Kahn © Andrey Burmakin - Fotolia.com
Akhenaten © Travis Hiner - Fotolia.com
Emperor Constantine © Elena Kovaleva - Fotolia.com
Caligula © Aaron Rutten - Fotolia.com
Ancient Jesus Christus Mosaic © philipus - Fotolia.com

DEDICATION

To the Aten

INTRODUCTION

Ancient Egypt, a civilization that until this day, astounds the modern man. Ancient Egyptians are most associated with their vast Pyramids and Temples. Very few go deeper to see that those monuments are just part and parcel of a greater aspiration of the Ancient Egyptian mind. We are often told that Ancient Egypt was a mysterious and magical land. This, I believe is mostly due to the uniqueness of the structures and language they left behind. Not many know, but we possess quite a bit of information about Ancient Egypt and the people who inhabited the great land. In fact, we may have more information about them than we do about other ancient people. Despite this, the mythology of Egypt remains firmly intact in the human imagination. In many ways, this is good for Egyptology, it garners interest. At the same time, it often trivializes Ancient Egypt as well. Ancient Egypt, was more; much more, than the monuments left behind.

It was a tremendous culture that stayed relatively intact for thousands of years despite going through long stretches of decline. Egyptians hated change and therefore, kept everything the same. Just look at the religion and art. It barely changed over the thousands of years of Ancient Egyptian history. That is, until Akhenaten arrived on to the scene. He was not the typical pharaoh; in fact, he wasn't meant to be pharaoh in the first place, but destiny had written him in to the historical narrative of the world.

He was to change everything about Egypt. Some have gone so far as to call him the heretic King. In this book, we will cover, ever so briefly, the life of Akhenaten, the Son of the Sun.

CHAPTER 1: THE HIDDEN SON

At around 1380 BC; Akhenaten, known as Amenhotep IV
before he reigned, was born to the great Pharaoh Amenhotep III
and his chief wife Tiye. Often the Pharaohs would have several
wives, but only one could be chief wife to the king. Tiye was
Amenhotep IIIs favorite. She was not of royal blood, in fact, she
was a commoner. But make no mistake about it, She was no
country bumpkin . Her Father was a wealthy land owner and
held several titles. She grew up well. Tiye bore Amenhotep III
6 children. 4 daughters and 2 sons. You would have never
known they had 6 children by the art he left behind. Most
depicted his wife and 5 children. His youngest son, Amenhotep
IV was missing from most of them. There is still debate as to the
reason, but as we progress in this book it might become very
clear why Amenhotep IV was omitted. He may have been ,
perhaps, an embarrassment to the royal family. The jury is still
out on this.

Amenhotep III built Egypt up quite high and there was no
stopping the Egyptian Juggernaut. In all fairness, he did inherit a
very strong Egypt from his predecessor. Regardless, he was no
slouch; his reign was relatively peaceful, and he knew how to
administer the country. He erected great statues and monuments.
He built so many that he is known to modern scholars to have

the most surviving statutes of any other king of Egypt to that point. It was clear, he was wealthy and in turn, it meant Egypt was doing very well. His eldest Son , Thutmose, was set to inherit the throne upon his passing. But as fate would have it, he died young. Amenhotep III had no choice, he had to make his " Hidden Son", Amenhotep IV, co-ruler and eventual successor to the throne. One would imagine he was not very happy about this at first. If he only knew what his son was going to do, Amenhotep III would have been spinning in his sarcophagus...

The hidden son was about to be revealed.

CHAPTER 2: THE ATEN GLEAMS

For the most part, Amenhotep III remained true to the main religious tradition of Egypt. Mainly the cult of Amen / Amun. He was very generous to the temples and during his reign, the religious institutions and the crown were slowly attaching at the hip. The Temple priests were at this time so wealthy they alone could exert quite a bit of influence on the affairs of Egypt. This was not expected to change, nor could anyone imagine that it would ever change. As stated earlier, Egyptians HATED change with a passion. Amenhotep IIIs successor was expected to stay in line and be okay with maintaining the status quo. There is some evidence that Amenhotep III tried to check some of the priesthoods power, but was generally not successful at this. That would change soon enough. Something was stirring behind the scenes; an old god was suddenly, but quietly, emerging from the sands of time.

Amenhotep III's chief wife; Tiye ,was an interesting woman. She refused to be what all Ancient Egyptian queens were supposed to be; an appendage to the Pharaoh . Don't get me wrong, women were treated fairly well in Ancient Egypt. However, there was a role to play and she, Queen Tiye, did not play it like most wives did at that time. It is said that no other Queen appeared so prominently in her husband's life. She was smart, strong and incredibly goal orientated. Her force of will gained her much admiration and respect from foreign dignitaries and kings. But there was one thing that was peculiar about her, a peculiarity that may have changed the course of history. She had unconventional religious views.

Often in Amenhotep III's reign, the Aten, an old god that existed in the Egyptian pantheon was venerated. Unlike the other gods, Aten was only depicted as the Sun disk. He did not have the head of any animal or human like the others did. Queen Tiye worshiped Aten, not to say she didn't worship other gods, but he was one of them and appeared prominent in her life. As a gift, Amenhotep III had a boat commissioned for her and named it " The Aten Gleams" . Clearly Aten was gaining prominence. It was in this environment that Amenhotep IV (Akhenaten) grew up in. Perhaps Tiye was teaching her young son about the Aten?

Eventually, Amenhotep III dies and his son Amenhotep IV becomes pharaoh around 1353-1350 BC...The Aten was about to rise on the horizon of Egyptian history.

CHAPTER 3: THE ATEN RISES

Amenhotep IV started out relatively well, he was crowned at Thebes as expected. He did what was expected of the inheritor to the throne. He got married to the beautiful Nerfertiti, the one whose bust is the face of Egypt to this day.

Picture of the Nefertiti bust in Neues Museum, Berlin. - Philip Pikart

(I would like to mention that although Nefertiti was Akhenatens chief wife. He did have a "lesser" wives, notably Kiya. She eventually bore Akhenaten his famous son Tutankhamun , who at the time was named Tutankhaten.)

In 1349 BC, He continued the many building projects his father left unfinished. Around this time his first daughter was born, Meritaten. He had commissioned the same kind of art the Egyptians had become used to seeing. So far, nothing was different, looks like he was going to be alright after all. Like father ,like son.

In 1348 BC, he commissioned 4 temples to the Aten at Karnak; he was starting to expand the Aten brand. At first this may have been slightly odd, but not terribly alarming. It certainly didn't look like he was trying to change the religion or anything like that. At least not yet. The priesthood and the Amen / Amun cult were still pretty strong, even unto his fourth year as Pharaoh. Everything was still status quo. Egypt was still a well-oiled machine.

In 1346 BC, work started on his new city **Akhetaten**. At this time he also managed to have 2 more daughters, Meketaten and Ankhenspaaten.

The irreparable break, was about to occur. More and more art was being commissioned that depicts either himself and or his family being blessed by the Aten.

*This image (or other media file) is in the [public domain](#) because its copyright has **expired**.*

Tension seemed to be mounting. In 1344 BC, he suddenly changes his name from Amenhotep (Amen is pleased) to Akhenaten (Servant to the Aten) . It was becoming clear that he was shifting away from the belief in many gods and focusing on the Aten. He is considered, in many ways , the first monotheist in history. Akhenaten eventually had enough of the old gods and their temples. He moved his throne to Amarna, 200 miles north of Thebes in 1342 BC. This action would be one of many that would eventually spur on Akhenaten's revolutionary new movement.

CHAPTER 4: THE REVOLUTION BEGINS

At Akhetaten, he would revolutionize everything the Egyptians held dear. He changed the art, the way buildings were built and above all, the religion. Slowly but surely, around 1341 BC, as his definition of the one true god Aten was being fleshed out, he started removing references to other gods. It got so bad that he went on a campaign to erase references to the other gods throughout Egypt, but most particularly the Amun. Oddly enough, many artifacts of the old religion were openly found at Amarna so it seems like he had a particularly hatred for Amun. Even some of his followers changed their names to reflect the new religion; adding Aten to their names. It is also not clear if he believed in an afterlife. There is no indication that he had any particular notion about what happens after death as did the pharaohs before and after him. This fact alone was revolutionary.

At this point, Akhenaten was in full revolt against the temples of Amun. Eventually, funding was cut off and temples were no longer able to function. You can imagine that several industries surrounding the traditional religious cult were shuttered as well.

As he got deeper into his reign, the art started to change dramatically. As a rule, Egyptians liked straight lines in their depictions of the gods and of people. In fact, the style of Egyptian art was beautiful but not as sophisticated as it may appear. Most of the paintings that are seen today were painted on a grid system and not free hand. In Akhenaten's time, it was freehand. But not only that, the style of art changed radically.

Most dramatically were the depictions of Akhenaten himself.

These are depictions that he commissioned on his own. They portray him with breasts, an elongated face ,limbs and a pot belly. His head was also elongated and his fingers were exceptionally long and spindly. He depicted his wife and kids in a similar way. Sometimes it was hard to tell the difference between the the pharaoh and Nefertiti. There are several theories as to why he was portrayed this way.

One of them being Incestuous intermarriage. This was very common practice amongst the royals of Egypt. Some have suggested that it simply caught up to them genetically. Another contingent believes he simply changed the art to be more dramatic. Despite the dramatic change in art, there are scenes you would never find in previous dynasties of Egypt and that is of warmth and intimacy. He has several pieces made displaying him , Nefertiti and his children enjoying each other's company. Hugging , kissing. The kids are sitting on Nefertiti's lap .

Nefertiti with Meketaten seated on her lap and Ankhesenpaaten leaning against her - : AnnekeBart

It's quite touching. It gives a glimpse into the personal life of the pharaoh that was never depicted in Egyptian art on that level before. The affection and warmth is breathtaking and when placed in contrast to the way the art usually was, it can move you to tears. Everything was shown either in its natural state or a bit aggregated. There was nothing blocky about Akhenaten's art. Whatever the true reason for the apparent deformities that show up on his statues, there is no doubt, the art was revolutionary for its time and incredibly taboo in contrast to the past. In 1337 BC, the last family portrait was carved showing all 6 daughters 3 of which were born in 1339 and 1338; Neferneferuaten, Neferneferure and Setepenre.

In addition, the building style changed as well. His temples and his city specifically were built with open spaces and expansive. They were meant to be abiding monuments to the Aten and the life giving rays that emanated from him.

In many ways, Akhenaten was a dreamer, he was artistic, wistful and was clearly religious. He proved time and time again that he was completely immersed in his new religion. In his divine reverie he would compose amazing verse. So much more passionate than much of what was written before him. He was quite a writer and composer, something we will discuss in the next chapter.

Chapter 5: In Praise of the Aten

Akhenaten was not only a religious visionary, he was quite a talented poet. Most of his poems and hymns, were dedicated to, not surprisingly, the Aten,. The one he is most famous for composing is the Great Hymn to the Aten. Egyptologist Toby Wilkinson said of it, "It has been called 'one of the most significant and splendid pieces of poetry to survive from the pre-Homeric world." - "The rise and Fall of Ancient Egypt".

Many people try to equate the verses of the hymn to similar verses found in the old testament, which was hundreds of years away. I think the theory is interesting, but I think the Hymn should be left to attest to its own glory. Often we lose the meaning of something when we try to compare it to other things. Some of the hymn is missing, but I think the Hymn of the Aten is a masterpiece just the way it is...I hope you agree.

The Great Hymn to the Aten:

A Hymn of praise of Her-aakhuti, the living one exalted in the Eastern Horizon in his name of Shu who is in the Aten, who liveth forever and ever, the living and great Aten, he who is in the Set-Festival, the lord of the Circle, the Lord of the Disk, the Lord of heaven, the Lord of earth, the lord of the House of the Aten in Aakhut-Aten, [of] the King of the South and the North, who liveth in Truth, lord of the Two Lands (i.e., Egypt), NEFER-KHEPERU-RA UA-EN-RA, the son of Ra, who liveth in Truth, Lord of Crowns, AAKHUN-ATEN, great in the period of his life, [and of] the great royal woman (or wife) whom he loveth, Lady of the Two Lands, NEFER-NEFERU-ATEN NEFERTITI, who liveth in health and youth for ever and ever.

He (i.e., Ai, a Fan-bearer and the Master of the King's Horse) saith: Thy rising [is] beautiful in the horizon of heaven, O Aten, ordainer of life. Thou dost shoot up in the horizon of the East, thou fillest every land with thy beneficence. Thou art beautiful and great and sparkling, and exalted above every land.. Thy arrows (i.e., rays) envelop (i.e., penetrate) everywhere all the lands which thou hast made.

Thou art as Ra. Thou bringest [them] according to their number, thou subduest them for thy beloved son. Thou thyself art afar off, but thy beams are upon the earth; thou art in their faces, they [admire] thy goings. Thou settest in the horizon of the west, the earth is in darkness, in the form of death. Men lie down in a booth wrapped up in cloths, one eye cannot see its fellow. If all their possessions, which are under their heads, be carried away they perceive it not.

Every lion emergeth from his lair, all the creeping things bite, darkness [is] a warm retreat (?). The land is in silence. He who made them hath set in his horizon. The earth becometh light, thou shootest up in the horizon, shining in the Aten in the day, thou scatterest the darkness. Thou sendest out thine arrows (i.e., rays), the Two Lands make festival, [men] wake up, stand upon their feet, it is thou who raisest them up. [They] wash their members, they take [their apparel] and array themselves therein, their hands are [stretched out] in praise at thy rising, throughout the land they do their works. Beasts and cattle of all kinds settle down upon the pastures, shrubs and vegetables flourish, the feathered fowl fly about over their marshes, their feathers praising thy Ka (person).

All the cattle rise up on their legs, creatures that fly and insects of all kinds spring into life, when thou risest up on them. The boats drop down and sail up the river, likewise every road openeth (or showeth itself) at thy rising, the fish in the river swim towards thy face, thy beams are in the depths of the Great Green (i.e., the Mediterranean and Red Seas). Thou makest offspring to take form in women, creating seed in men. Thou makest the son to live in the womb of his mother, making him to be quiet that he crieth not; thou art a nurse in the womb, giving breath to vivify that which he hath made. [When] he droppeth from the womb ... on the day of his birth [he] openeth his mouth in the [ordinary] manner, thou providest his sustenance.

The young bird in the egg speaketh in the shell, thou givest breath to him inside it to make him to live. Thou makest for him his mature form so that he can crack the shell [being] inside the egg. He cometh forth from the egg, he chirpeth with all his might, when he hath come forth from it (the egg), he walketh on his two feet. O how many are the things which thou hast made! They are hidden from the face, O thou

One God, like whom there is no other. Thou didst create the earth by thy heart (or will), thou alone existing, men and women, cattle, beasts of every kind that are upon the earth, and that move upon feet (or legs), all the creatures that are in the sky and that fly with their wings, [and] the deserts of Syria and Kesh (Nubia), and the Land of Egypt.

Thou settest every person in his place. Thou providest their daily food, every man having the portion allotted to him, [thou] dost compute the duration of his life. Their tongues are different in speech, their characteristics (or forms), and likewise their skins [in colour], giving distinguishing marks to the dwellers in foreign lands. Thou makest Hapi (the Nile) in the Tuat (Underworld), thou bringest it when thou wishest to make mortals to live, inasmuch as thou hast made them for thyself, their Lord who dost support them to the uttermost, O thou Lord of every land, thou shinest upon them, O ATEN of the day, thou great one of majesty. Thou makest the life of all remote lands. Thou settest a Nile in heaven, which cometh down to them.

It maketh a flood on the mountains like the Great Green Sea, it maketh to be watered their fields in their villages. How beneficent are thy plans, O Lord of Eternity! A Nile in heaven art thou for the dwellers in the foreign lands (or deserts), and for all the beasts of the desert that go upon feet (or legs). Hapi (the Nile) cometh from the Tuat for the land of Egypt. Thy beams nourish every field; thou risest up [and] they live, they germinate for thee. Thou makest the Seasons to develop everything that thou hast made:

The season of Pert (i.e., Nov. 16-March 16) so that they may refresh themselves, and the season Heh (i.e., March 16-Nov. 16) in order to taste thee. 1 Thou hast made the heaven which is remote that thou mayest shine therein and look upon everything that thou hast made. Thy being is one, thou shinest (or, shootest up) among thy creatures as the LIVING ATEN, rising, shining, departing afar off, returning. Thou hast made millions of creations (or, evolutions) from thy one self (viz.) towns and cities, villages, fields, roads and river. Every eye (i.e., all men) beholdeth thee confronting it. Thou art the Aten of the day at its zenith.

At thy departure thine eye ... thou didst create their faces so that thou mightest not see. ... ONE thou didst make ... Thou art in my heart. There is no other who knoweth thee except thy son Nefer-kheperu-Ra Ua-en-Ra. Thou hast made him wise to understand thy plans [and] thy power. The earth came into being by thy hand, even as thou hast created them (i.e., men). Thou risest, they live; thou settest, they die. As for thee, there is duration of life in thy members, life is in thee. [All] eyes [gaze upon] thy beauties until thou settest, [when] all labours are relinquished. Thou settest in the West, thou risest, making to flourish ... for the King. Every man who [standeth on his] foot, since thou didst lay the foundation of the earth, thou hast raised up for thy son who came forth from thy body, the King of the South and the North, Living in Truth, Lord of Crowns, Aakhun-Aten, great in the duration of his life [and for] the Royal Wife, great of majesty, Lady of the Two Lands, Nefer-neferu-Aten Nefertiti, living [and] young forever and ever.

The source of the hymn:

TUTANKHAMEN
AMENISM, ATENISM AND EGYPTIAN MONOTHEISM

by E.A.W. Budge

CHAPTER 6: WHAT HAVE I DONE TO THE KING MY LORD?

Pharaohs were not just supreme rulers of Egypt, they were also expected to be great warriors as well. Akhenaten broke with this tradition. He did not appear to be interested in the military at all. This put Egypt in grave peril. He inherited a strong Egypt with many alliances across much of the middle east. With his disinterest, Egyptian clout was starting to wane. During this time, Canaan and surrounding areas were constantly under attack by tribes people. For the most part, pharaohs would quell these, but Akhenaten didn't seem to care.

We know this from a series of tablets called the "Amarna Tablets" Or " Amarna letters". These letters were discovered in 1887, by a village woman looking to farm a piece of land. There are just under 400 letters that we know of, but it is highly probable that many have been destroyed over time. Many of the Amarna letters are to Akhenaten from various allies and supporters of Egypt in Canaan (Modern day Israel) and Amurru (Modern day Syria and Lebanon). The letters were written in Akkadian cuneiform as opposed to Egyptian. This shouldn't be too surprising because that was the language of diplomacy during this time. It would be expected that Akhenaten would have translators at his disposal.

Many of these letters take a rather dire tone. A good deal of them show that Akhenaten was not responsive to his diplomats or allies. There were warnings of insurgencies and incursions against lands either controlled by Egypt or allies of Egypt. Akhenaten's seeming disregard stunned some of these foreign leaders. Several of them sent more than one letter. Some leaders were distraught by this and begged Akhenaten for help. Often they wondered if they in some way insulted the pharaoh. But no, he was not insulted. He was a mystic, a religious revolutionary. His mind was simply not into it. It is not to say that Egypt lost all its military clout, there is some evidence that some activity was taking place. For the most part, Egypt was losing face fast. This, however, would not last.

CHAPTER 7: THE ATEN SETS

This new way of doing things was inevitably going to catch up with Akhenaten. He did not have the support of the general population, nor the priesthood. Although he was the rightful Pharaoh, and had followers, he did not have all of Egypt and therefore, it was not sustainable. Before his reign was to come to an end however, he was beset by numerous personal tragedies.

In 1336 BC, his second born, Meketaten died. About a year later his famous wife Nefertiti dies as well. There is some evidence that she kept things together for Akhenaten and thus, her death was a severe blow. In 1335 BC, after she died, he took his firstborn daughter Meritaten as Queen. This might sound sick to us in today's society, but this was not unusual in Ancient Egypt. But then a year later, a figure by the name of Smenkhkare comes on to the scene and eventually marries Meritaten. It is not clear who Smenkhkare was. Some say it was simply Nefertiti recast as a man. The reason some say this is because there are scenes of Akhenaten and Smenkhkare that seem a bit intimate. Another possibility that is floating out there is that Smenkhkare may have been a male lover to Akhenaten. Others say it was Akhenaten's son or brother in law. The jury is still out on who this person was. One thing is for sure, Smenkhkare became co-regent with Akhenaten.

In 1332 BC, Akhenaten died, as did Smenkhkare . With Akenahten's death, his religious revolution died out very quickly. The city he built was also hastily abandoned. Despite the obvious reason for its abandonment, there is also evidence there was a plague in the region and that may have hastened the abandonment as well.

Akhenaten was so reviled for what he did, the priests had all his temples disassembled. They wanted to erase any trace of this heretic king. Many of the stones were simply recycled and used in other building projects. Akhenaten's images were taken down and the inscriptions to the Aten were defaced.

His son, the famous King Tutankhamun (King Tut) was his successor and was depicted as a liberator of the Egyptian people. A liberator from his father's cursed memory. King Tutankhamun was only 9 years old at the time. He was raised in a "monotheistic" household so it is unlikely he chose to go back to the old ways of Ancient Egyptian religion. He was probably sheltered from it as he grew up. King Tutankhamun was lore likely a pawn of the powerful priests of Amun. No matter what beliefs he had in his soul, he did reinstate the old time religious practices and had many great monuments built to the gods.

At the young age of 20, King Tutankhamun would die and even he was expunged from the history of Egypt. Essentially everyone associated with Akhenaten was expunged from ancient history as if they did not exist. If you look at the kings lists, they are not mentioned. It goes from his father Amenhotep III right to Pharaoh Haremheb, the successor to King Tutankhamun.

Akhenaten was destined to be forgotten forever. That is until the late nineteenth century when he was rediscovered thanks to the traces of his reign that were not destroyed.

As quickly as the Aten rose across the horizon of Ancient Egypt, it set. Thus concluded the reign of the most controversial figure in ancient Egyptian history. So controversial was he that his memory would outlast all his enemies.

CONCLUSION

Akhenaten was clearly a great figure. Not so much for what he accomplished or failed to accomplish, but great because he tried to change how things worked. He attempted to innovate, to disrupt the status quo. Although his great revolution failed, he made a great impact on history. Although this might sound controversial, it is said that he was the first monotheist in history. This idea is so prevalent that many books have been written about this. Some are a bit out there and some make very cogent points.

Whether he was the first monotheist or not, one thing is clear. Historians and religious scholars cannot ignore his influence. They can try, but the Aten will always loom large on the horizon.

ABOUT THE AUTHOR

D.M. Alon is a bestselling author of 50books, in 6 different genres and founder of Numinosity Press Inc.

He writes on a wide variety of topics. His conversational writing style and his ability to convert the esoteric into the mundane is his specialty; this has gained him popularity in the genres that he writes for.

Please feel free to email him at
DMAlon@interviewswithhistory.com

Amazon Author Page: www.amazon.com/author/dmalon

ABOUT THE INTERVIEWS WITH HISTORY SERIES

The goal of the Interviews With History series is to provide concise biographical information for people who want to read biographies, but do not have the time to read hundreds of pages or purchase expensive study courses. What you read in an Interviews With History Titles are the pertinent facts; no filler. Written in an easy to understand and conversational fashion. To learn about future releases in this series please visit www.interviewswithhistory.com

BIBLIOGRAPHY

"The Rise and Fall of Ancient Egypt". - **Toby Wilkinson**

TUTANKHAMEN -AMENISM, ATENISM AND EGYPTIAN MONOTHEISM

By E.A.W. Budge

Akhenaten The Heretic King -

Akhenaten King of Egypt -